Table Of Contents

**Chapter 1 Introduction to the
Changing Landscape of Interviews**   5

The Evolution of Job Interviews in
the Digital Age   5

Understanding the Impact of
Technology on Interviewing
Processes   7

The Importance of Adaptability for
Career Changers   10

**Chapter 2 Preparing for the 2024
Interview**   12

Identifying Transferable Skills and
Experience   12

Crafting a Compelling Career
Change Narrative   15

Researching the Industry and
Company   17

Developing a Strong Personal
Brand   20

**Chapter 3 Mastering the Virtual
Interview**   22

Embracing Video Interviewing Platforms 22

Setting Up a Professional Virtual Interview Environment 25

Overcoming Challenges and Technical Difficulties 27

Showcasing Nonverbal Communication in a Virtual Setting 30

Chapter 4 Navigating the AI-Driven Interview Process 33

Understanding AI-Based Applicant Tracking Systems 33

Optimizing Your Resume and Application for AI Screening 36

Leveraging AI Platforms for Interview Preparation 38

Demonstrating Your Skills and Abilities to AI Interviewers 40

Chapter 5 Cracking the Behavioral Interview Code 42

Analyzing Common Behavioral Interview Questions 43

Crafting Effective STAR Responses 45

Showcasing Transferable Skills
and Experience   47

Handling Situational and
Hypothetical Questions   50

Chapter 6 Showcasing Your Value
through Case Studies and
Simulations   52

The Role of Case Studies and
Simulations in Interviews   52

Understanding the Purpose and
Format of Case Studies   55

Approaching Case Studies with
Confidence and Analytical Thinking   57

Demonstrating Problem-Solving
Skills through Simulations   59

Chapter 7 Nailing the Final Interview
and Negotiating Offers   62

Preparing for the Final Interview
Round   62

Showcasing Your Fit with the
Company Culture   64

Handling Salary Negotiations and
Benefits Discussions   66

Evaluating Multiple Offers and
Making an Informed Decision   69
Chapter 8 Succeeding in the New
Role and Beyond   71
Onboarding and Transitioning into
the New Career   71
Building Relationships and
Establishing a Professional Network   73
Continuously Developing Skills
and Knowledge   76
Embracing Lifelong Learning and
Adaptability   78
Chapter 9 Cracking the 2024
Interview Code   80
Reflecting on the Journey of
Career Change   80
Embracing the Skills and
Strategies for Future Success   83
Continuing to Evolve in an Ever-
Changing Job Market   85

Chapter 1
Introduction to the Changing Landscape of Interviews

The Evolution of Job Interviews in the Digital Age

In today's fast-paced and technologically advanced world, the job interview process has undergone a significant transformation. With the advent of the digital age, career changers must adapt to the changing landscape of interviewing in 2024. This subchapter explores the evolution of job interviews and offers valuable insights for those navigating the digital interviewing realm.

The digital age has revolutionized the way employers and candidates connect. Traditional face-to-face interviews have gradually given way to virtual interviews conducted through video conferencing platforms. This shift has not only streamlined the hiring process but has also opened up opportunities for career changers to showcase their skills and expertise from anywhere in the world.

One of the key advantages of digital interviews is their convenience. Instead of traveling long distances for an in-person interview, candidates can now participate in interviews from the comfort of their own homes. This flexibility allows career changers to explore job opportunities in different geographical locations without the logistical challenges that were once associated with interviews.

However, with the convenience of digital interviews comes the challenge of adapting to new technologies. Career changers must become well-versed in video conferencing platforms, ensuring they have a stable internet connection, appropriate lighting, and a professional background. Additionally, mastering non-verbal communication cues, such as maintaining eye contact with the camera, becomes crucial in making a positive impression on potential employers.

Furthermore, the digital age has witnessed the rise of artificial intelligence (AI) in the hiring process. Many companies now use AI-powered software to screen resumes, conduct initial interviews, and even assess candidates' facial expressions and tone of voice. Career changers must optimize their resumes and online profiles to ensure they are compatible with these AI systems and showcase their relevant skills effectively.

As technology continues to advance, the future of job interviews may involve virtual reality (VR) and augmented reality (AR) simulations. These immersive experiences can provide employers with a better understanding of a candidate's abilities and potential fit within the organization. Career changers must stay abreast of these emerging technologies and be prepared to adapt to new interview formats.

The digital age has brought about a significant evolution in the job interview process. Career changers must embrace the convenience and opportunities presented by digital interviews while also familiarizing themselves with the technologies and tools used in this new era. By staying informed and adaptable, career changers can crack the 2024 interview code and confidently navigate the changing landscape of job interviews in the digital age.

Understanding the Impact of Technology on Interviewing Processes

In today's rapidly evolving digital landscape, technology has revolutionized various aspects of our lives, including the way we conduct job interviews. As a career changer, it is crucial to stay updated on the latest advancements and understand the impact of technology on interviewing processes in 2024 and beyond.

One of the most significant changes brought about by technology is the rise of virtual interviews. With the advent of video conferencing tools and platforms, employers can now connect with candidates from anywhere in the world, eliminating the need for expensive and time-consuming travel. Virtual interviews offer convenience, flexibility, and cost-effectiveness for both employers and job seekers.

However, it is essential to adapt your interviewing skills to the virtual format. Familiarize yourself with the technology beforehand, ensuring that your internet connection and audiovisual equipment are of high quality. Dress professionally, choose a quiet and well-lit location, and maintain eye contact with your interviewer by looking into the camera. Practicing virtual interviews with friends or family can help you become more comfortable with the format.

Another technology-driven change in interviewing processes is the utilization of artificial intelligence (AI) in screening candidates. Many companies now use AI-powered software to analyze resumes, assess skills, and even conduct initial interviews. As a career changer, it is crucial to optimize your resume for AI systems by incorporating relevant keywords and tailoring it to each job application. Moreover, be prepared for AI-driven interviews by familiarizing yourself with common interview questions and practicing concise and well-structured responses.

In 2024, the use of AI may extend to facial recognition and sentiment analysis during interviews. Some companies are experimenting with AI algorithms that can analyze facial expressions, body language, and vocal tones to gauge a candidate's suitability for a role. As a career changer, it is essential to be mindful of your non-verbal cues during interviews and ensure that your body language aligns with your words.

Lastly, technology has also influenced the post-interview stage. Many employers now use applicant tracking systems (ATS) to manage and evaluate candidate applications. These systems scan resumes and cover letters for keywords and qualifications, ranking candidates based on relevance. To increase your chances of success, tailor your application materials to match the job requirements and use industry-specific keywords.

As a career changer, it is crucial to understand and adapt to the impact of technology on interviewing processes in 2024. Embrace virtual interviews, optimize your resume for AI screening, be mindful of your non-verbal cues, and tailor your application materials to increase your chances of success. By staying informed and leveraging technology to your advantage, you can crack the 2024 interview code and make a successful career transition.

The Importance of Adaptability for Career Changers

In today's fast-paced and ever-changing job market, adaptability has become a critical skill for individuals looking to make a successful career change. As the world evolves, new technologies, industries, and job roles are constantly emerging, making it essential for career changers to be able to adapt and navigate these changes effectively.

One of the key reasons why adaptability is so important for career changers is that it allows individuals to stay relevant and competitive in their chosen field. With the rapid advancements in technology and automation, many traditional job roles are becoming obsolete or evolving into new and different positions. By being adaptable, career changers can quickly learn new skills, embrace emerging technologies, and position themselves as valuable assets to potential employers.

Moreover, adaptability enables career changers to overcome challenges and setbacks that may arise during the transition period. Changing careers can be a daunting task, and it's not uncommon to face obstacles along the way. However, those who possess adaptability are more likely to bounce back from setbacks, learn from their experiences, and forge ahead with renewed determination. This ability to adapt and persevere in the face of adversity is highly valued by employers and can significantly enhance a career changer's prospects.

Adaptability also opens up new opportunities for career changers. By being open to change and willing to explore different paths, individuals can discover hidden talents and interests they never knew they had. This flexibility allows career changers to explore diverse industries and job roles, ultimately leading them to find a career that aligns with their skills, passions, and values.

When it comes to interviewing in 2024, adaptability will be even more crucial. The job market is expected to undergo significant transformations, driven by advancements in artificial intelligence and automation. As a result, interviewers will be looking for candidates who can demonstrate their ability to adapt to these changes. By highlighting their past experiences of successfully navigating career transitions and showcasing their willingness to learn and grow, career changers can position themselves as desirable candidates in the eyes of potential employers.

Adaptability is a vital skill for career changers in today's rapidly changing job market. By embracing change, overcoming challenges, and being open to new opportunities, career changers can enhance their prospects and find success in their chosen field. In the context of interviewing in 2024, adaptability will be highly valued by employers, making it essential for career changers to develop and showcase this skill.

Chapter 2
Preparing for the 2024 Interview

Identifying Transferable Skills and Experience

In today's fast-paced and ever-changing job market, career changers face unique challenges when it comes to interviewing in 2024. As industries evolve and new technologies emerge, it is crucial for individuals looking to transition into a new field to identify their transferable skills and experiences. This subchapter of "Cracking the 2024 Interview Code - A Guide for Career Changers" is dedicated to helping career changers recognize and leverage their existing skills and experiences to ace their interviews.

Transferable skills are those abilities that can be applied across different industries or job roles. They are not specific to a particular field but are valuable assets that can be carried from one career to another. Identifying these skills is the first step towards a successful career change. In this subchapter, we will explore various techniques to recognize and highlight transferable skills during interviews.

One effective strategy is to conduct a self-assessment. Take the time to reflect on your previous roles and responsibilities, and identify the skills you have acquired. These could include communication, problem-solving, leadership, teamwork, or project management skills, among others. By understanding how your skills can be transferred to a new industry, you can confidently showcase your abilities during interviews.

Another approach is to seek feedback from colleagues, mentors, or supervisors who have worked closely with you. They can provide insights into your strengths and skills that you may not have realized or considered valuable. Incorporating this feedback into your self-assessment can strengthen your understanding of your transferable skills and enhance your interview performance.

Furthermore, it is essential to connect your transferable skills and experiences to the specific needs of the industry or job you are pursuing. Research the target field to identify the skills highly sought after by employers. Tailor your resume and interview responses to emphasize how your existing skills align with the requirements of the new role. This will demonstrate your adaptability and make you a compelling candidate in the eyes of the interviewer.

Identifying and effectively communicating your transferable skills and experiences can significantly impact your success as a career changer in the 2024 job market. By conducting self-assessments, seeking feedback, and aligning your skills with industry demands, you are positioning yourself as a valuable asset to potential employers. "Cracking the 2024 Interview Code - A Guide for Career Changers" provides further guidance and practical tips on leveraging your transferable skills to ace interviews and successfully transition into a new career.

Crafting a Compelling Career Change Narrative

In the ever-evolving professional landscape of 2024, career changers face unique challenges when it comes to interviewing for new opportunities. Navigating this terrain requires careful preparation and a compelling career change narrative that showcases your skills, experiences, and motivations. This subchapter will guide you through the process of crafting a powerful narrative that will captivate interviewers and set you apart from the competition.

When embarking on a career change, it is essential to understand the reasons behind your decision. Reflect on your motivations and aspirations, and identify the transferable skills you possess that are relevant to your desired field. This self-reflection will serve as the foundation for your narrative, allowing you to articulate a clear and authentic story during interviews.

Start by highlighting the experiences and achievements from your previous career that directly correlate with the new path you are pursuing. Emphasize the skills you have developed, such as leadership, problem-solving, or project management, and demonstrate how they can be effectively applied in the new industry. By showcasing your transferable skills, you will assure potential employers of your ability to make a seamless transition.

It is also crucial to address any gaps in your experience or knowledge that may arise due to the career change. Be prepared to explain how you plan to bridge these gaps, whether through further education, training, or self-directed learning. This proactive approach showcases your commitment to professional growth and adaptability, traits highly valued in the dynamic job market of 2024.

Additionally, consider incorporating personal anecdotes that highlight your passion and dedication to the new field. Share instances where you went above and beyond to acquire new skills or demonstrated a keen interest in the industry. These stories will leave a lasting impression on interviewers, showcasing your genuine excitement for the career change.

Finally, practice delivering your narrative with confidence and clarity. Anticipate potential questions and rehearse concise and compelling responses. Incorporate your career change narrative into your elevator pitch, allowing you to confidently articulate your story in any professional setting.

Crafting a compelling career change narrative is essential to succeed in the competitive job market of 2024. By showcasing your transferable skills, addressing any knowledge gaps, incorporating personal anecdotes, and practicing your delivery, you will be well-equipped to captivate interviewers and secure the opportunities you seek. Embrace the power of your unique journey and let your narrative shine.

Researching the Industry and Company

When it comes to interview preparation, one of the most crucial steps for career changers is researching the industry and company they are applying to. In the rapidly evolving job market of 2024, staying updated and well-informed about the industry trends and the specific organization you are targeting can give you a competitive edge.

To begin your research, start by understanding the broader industry landscape. Look for recent reports, articles, or studies that highlight the key trends, challenges, and opportunities in the industry. Pay attention to any technological advancements, regulatory changes, or market disruptions that may impact the sector. By familiarizing yourself with the industry's current state, you will be better equipped to discuss these topics confidently during your interview.

Next, delve into the specific company you are interviewing with. Begin by exploring their official website to gain insights into their mission, values, and organizational culture. Check out their products or services, target audience, and any recent news or press releases. This will help you understand the company's positioning, goals, and overall direction.

Additionally, leverage social media platforms to gain further knowledge about the company. Many organizations have active social media accounts where they share updates, industry news, and engage with their audience. Follow their accounts on platforms such as LinkedIn, Twitter, or Instagram to stay in the loop and get a sense of their brand personality.

It's also important to research the company's competitors. Understanding how the organization differentiates itself from its rivals can provide valuable insights during the interview process. Look for information about the competitor's strengths, weaknesses, and market share. This knowledge can help you formulate intelligent questions and demonstrate your industry awareness during the interview.

Lastly, consider connecting with professionals in the industry or employees working within the company. LinkedIn is a great platform to network and reach out to individuals who can provide valuable insights and firsthand experiences. Conduct informational interviews to gather more information about the industry and the specific company you are targeting.

By conducting thorough research on the industry and company you are applying to, you will be well-prepared to discuss relevant topics, showcase your enthusiasm, and align your skills and experiences with their needs. This level of preparation will not only impress the interviewer but also demonstrate your commitment to making a successful career change in the dynamic landscape of 2024.

Developing a Strong Personal Brand

In today's rapidly changing job market, it has become increasingly important for career changers to develop a strong personal brand. With the advancements in technology and the rise of social media, employers are now looking beyond traditional qualifications and focusing more on an individual's personal brand. This subchapter aims to guide career changers on how to build and showcase their personal brand effectively in the context of interviewing in 2024.

First and foremost, it is essential to understand what personal branding entails. Your personal brand is the unique combination of skills, experiences, and values that sets you apart from other candidates. It is the image you project to potential employers and the impression they have of you. Developing a personal brand requires self-reflection and a deep understanding of your strengths, passions, and career goals.

To start building your personal brand, consider conducting a thorough self-assessment. Identify your core skills, experiences, and values that align with your desired career path. This introspection will help you articulate your unique selling points and differentiate yourself from other candidates. Additionally, researching industry trends and anticipating the skills required in 2024 will enable you to align your personal brand with future job market demands.

In the digital age, having a strong online presence is crucial. Create a professional website or portfolio that showcases your work, achievements, and career aspirations. Leverage social media platforms like LinkedIn to network with professionals in your desired field and share relevant content. Engaging in online discussions and posting thought leadership articles will establish your credibility and expertise.

Networking remains a powerful tool for career changers. Attend industry events, join professional organizations, and reach out to individuals who can offer guidance and support. Building relationships with professionals in your field of interest can open doors to opportunities and help you stay updated on industry trends.

Lastly, personal branding requires consistent self-promotion. Be proactive in sharing your accomplishments, whether it's through updating your resume, creating a compelling elevator pitch, or leveraging testimonials from mentors or colleagues. Use storytelling techniques to effectively communicate your unique experiences and the value you bring to potential employers.

Developing a strong personal brand is essential for career changers in the context of interviewing in 2024. By conducting a self-assessment, building a strong online presence, networking effectively, and consistently promoting yourself, you can differentiate yourself from other candidates and position yourself as a valuable asset to prospective employers. Embrace the power of personal branding and unlock new opportunities for a successful career transition in the rapidly evolving job market.

Chapter 3
Mastering the Virtual Interview

Embracing Video Interviewing Platforms

In today's rapidly evolving job market, technology is changing the way we conduct interviews. The emergence of video interviewing platforms has revolutionized the hiring process, offering a convenient and efficient way for both employers and candidates to connect. As a career changer, it is crucial to stay updated with the latest trends in interviewing, and embracing video interviewing platforms is a must in 2024.

Video interviewing platforms enable candidates to showcase their skills and personality through virtual interviews, eliminating the need for costly and time-consuming in-person meetings. These platforms provide a range of features, such as face-to-face video interviews, pre-recorded interviews, and even AI-powered assessments. By utilizing these tools, career changers can overcome geographic barriers and compete on a global scale, expanding their job opportunities like never before.

One of the key advantages of video interviewing platforms is the flexibility they offer. As a career changer, you may have commitments or responsibilities that make it challenging to attend in-person interviews. With video interviewing, you can schedule interviews at a time that suits you best, allowing for better work-life balance and increased convenience.

Additionally, video interviews can help you stand out from the competition. By leveraging the visual medium, you can engage interviewers in a more dynamic and memorable way. You can use visual aids, such as slides or portfolios, to showcase your achievements, skills, and projects. With the right preparation and presentation, you can leave a lasting impression on interviewers, increasing your chances of landing your desired job.

While video interviewing platforms offer numerous benefits, it is essential to prepare thoroughly to ensure success. Practice answering common interview questions, practice using the platform's features, and test your internet connection and audiovisual equipment to avoid any technical glitches. Dress professionally and create a distraction-free environment for your interview. Remember, just because the interview is virtual, it doesn't mean you should treat it any less seriously than an in-person interview.

As a career changer, embracing video interviewing platforms is a crucial step in cracking the 2024 interview code. By familiarizing yourself with these platforms and utilizing their features effectively, you can enhance your chances of securing your desired career transition. Stay up to date with the latest trends and technologies in interviewing, and you'll be well-prepared to navigate the ever-changing job market of the future. Embrace the video interviewing revolution and take control of your career change journey.

Setting Up a Professional Virtual Interview Environment

In the rapidly evolving job market of 2024, virtual interviews have become the norm. As a career changer, it is vital to adapt to this new mode of interviewing to increase your chances of success. Creating a professional virtual interview environment not only showcases your technical proficiency but also demonstrates your commitment to professionalism and adaptability. Here are some essential tips to help you set up an impressive virtual interview environment.

1. Choose the Right Location - Select a quiet, well-lit area of your home where you can conduct the interview without interruptions or distractions. Ensure that the background is clean and clutter-free, as it reflects your attention to detail and organization.

2. Test Your Equipment - Prior to the interview, test your computer, webcam, and microphone to ensure they are working correctly. Familiarize yourself with the video conferencing platform being used and make sure you have a stable internet connection. Being technologically prepared will help you avoid any technical glitches during the interview.

3. Dress Professionally - Just because the interview is virtual doesn't mean you can compromise on your appearance. Dress as you would for an in-person interview, wearing professional attire that reflects the company's culture. Looking professional will help you feel more confident and make a positive impression on the interviewer.

4. Pay Attention to Lighting and Framing - Good lighting is crucial for a clear and visible video feed. Position yourself facing a natural light source, such as a window, to illuminate your face. Avoid sitting with your back to a window as it can make you appear shadowy. Additionally, ensure that the camera is positioned at eye level and that you are centered in the frame.

5. Minimize Distractions - Inform your household members about the interview beforehand to ensure they do not disturb you during the process. Put your mobile phone on silent mode and close any unnecessary applications on your computer. Create a professional atmosphere by eliminating background noise and interruptions.

6. Prepare Your Interview Space - Have a pen, notepad, and a copy of your resume readily available. This will allow you to take notes, refer to key points, and jot down any questions you may have during the interview. Being organized and well-prepared showcases your dedication and attention to detail.

By following these tips, you will be able to create a professional virtual interview environment that impresses potential employers and helps you stand out in the competitive job market of 2024. Remember, adapting to new technologies and staying ahead of the curve is crucial for career changers, and mastering the art of virtual interviewing is a valuable skill to possess. Good luck with your future interviews!

Overcoming Challenges and Technical Difficulties

In the fast-paced world of 2024, the job market is constantly evolving, and so are the interviewing techniques. As a career changer, you may find yourself facing unique challenges and technical difficulties during the interview process. However, with the right mindset and preparation, you can overcome these obstacles and land your dream job. This subchapter aims to equip you with strategies to navigate through these challenges and come out on top.

One of the most significant challenges career changers face is bridging the gap between their previous experience and the requirements of the new field. It's essential to highlight transferable skills and demonstrate how they can be applied to the new role. Research the industry thoroughly, identify the skills and knowledge required, and showcase how your background aligns with those requirements. By presenting a compelling case for your suitability, you can overcome any doubts the interviewer may have.

Technical difficulties can also hinder the interviewing process, especially in the technology-driven era of 2024. With virtual interviews becoming the norm, it's crucial to be well-versed in video conferencing platforms and have a reliable internet connection. Prior to the interview, test your equipment, ensure proper lighting, and eliminate any potential distractions. Familiarize yourself with the platform's features, such as screen sharing, to effectively present your portfolio or any other relevant materials.

Another challenge career changers may encounter is adapting to new interview formats. In 2024, traditional interviews are gradually being replaced by innovative techniques such as behavioral and situational interviews. Prepare for these by researching common questions, practicing your responses, and aligning them with the company's values and culture. Additionally, consider seeking out mock interview opportunities or working with a career coach who can provide valuable feedback and guidance.

Lastly, as a career changer, you might face skepticism from interviewers who question your commitment to the new field. Address this concern directly by explaining your motivation for the change and showcasing any relevant experiences or certifications you have acquired. Demonstrate your passion, willingness to learn, and adaptability to convince the interviewer of your dedication.

In conclusion, while career changers may face unique challenges and technical difficulties when interviewing in 2024, it is possible to overcome them with the right strategies. By emphasizing transferable skills, mastering technical aspects, adapting to new interview formats, and addressing any doubts about your commitment, you can position yourself as a strong candidate. Remember to stay confident, stay prepared, and stay focused on your goal of cracking the 2024 interview code.

Showcasing Nonverbal Communication in a Virtual Setting

In today's rapidly evolving job market, virtual interviews have become the new norm. As a career changer looking to make a lasting impression, it is crucial to understand how to effectively showcase your nonverbal communication skills in a virtual setting. With advancements in technology, employers are increasingly relying on virtual interviews to assess candidates' suitability for a role. To crack the 2024 interview code, you must master the art of nonverbal communication through a screen.

First and foremost, it is essential to create a professional and engaging virtual environment. Choose a well-lit space with minimal distractions, and ensure that your background is neat and professional. This will not only project a positive image but also demonstrate your attention to detail and organizational skills.

Next, pay attention to your body language. Nonverbal cues such as facial expressions, eye contact, and posture can convey confidence, enthusiasm, and interest. Maintain eye contact by looking directly into the camera, as this creates a sense of connection with the interviewer. Sit up straight and avoid fidgeting, as it shows professionalism and attentiveness.

Gestures can also play a significant role in virtual interviews. Use your hands purposefully to emphasize key points or to show engagement. However, be mindful of excessive movements, as they can be distracting. Practice using gestures naturally and sparingly to enhance your communication.

Vocal tone and pace are crucial aspects of nonverbal communication. Speak clearly and at a moderate pace, as this will ensure your words are easily understood. Vary your tone to convey enthusiasm and interest, but avoid sounding monotone or overly animated.

Furthermore, dressing appropriately is equally important in a virtual setting. Dress professionally from head to toe, as this not only boosts your confidence but also shows respect for the interviewer and the interview process. Remember, even though you are not physically present, your appearance still matters.

Lastly, remember to be attentive and responsive during the virtual interview. Active listening is an essential nonverbal skill that demonstrates your interest and engagement. Nodding, smiling, and using appropriate verbal cues such as "yes," "I understand," or "great point" can enhance your nonverbal communication and build rapport with the interviewer.

Mastering nonverbal communication in a virtual setting is vital for career changers navigating the world of interviewing in 2024. By creating a professional environment, being mindful of body language, utilizing appropriate gestures, maintaining a pleasant vocal tone, dressing professionally, and being attentive and responsive, you can effectively showcase your nonverbal communication skills and leave a lasting impression on potential employers. Remember, in the virtual world, nonverbal communication is just as important as verbal communication.

Chapter 4
Navigating the AI-Driven Interview Process

Understanding AI-Based Applicant Tracking Systems

In today's rapidly evolving job market, it is crucial for career changers to understand the role of AI-based applicant tracking systems (ATS) in the hiring process. As technology continues to advance, recruiters are increasingly relying on these systems to streamline the recruitment process and identify the most qualified candidates. Therefore, it is imperative for career changers to familiarize themselves with how these systems work and how they can optimize their resumes to increase their chances of getting hired in 2024.

AI-based applicant tracking systems are software applications that automate the initial screening and filtering of resumes. They use AI algorithms to analyze and categorize resumes based on specific keywords, skills, and qualifications. This enables recruiters to quickly identify the most relevant candidates for a particular job opening, saving them time and effort in the shortlisting process.

For career changers, understanding how ATS works is essential for tailoring their resumes effectively. To optimize their chances of getting through the initial screening, career changers should incorporate relevant keywords and phrases related to their target industry or job role. By aligning their skills and qualifications with the requirements mentioned in the job description, career changers can increase their chances of being shortlisted by the AI-based ATS.

Additionally, it is crucial for career changers to format their resumes in a way that is easily readable by ATS. This means using standard fonts, headings, and bullet points to ensure that the system can accurately extract and analyze the information provided. Avoiding complex graphics, tables, or images is also recommended, as these elements can confuse the system and potentially lead to the rejection of the resume.

Furthermore, career changers should consider incorporating a skills section in their resumes to highlight transferable skills and relevant certifications. This section should include keywords and phrases that are commonly used in the target industry to further catch the attention of the AI-based ATS.

Understanding AI-based applicant tracking systems is vital for career changers who want to succeed in the job market of 2024. By optimizing their resumes with relevant keywords, tailoring their skills section, and formatting their resumes appropriately, career changers can increase their chances of getting through the initial screening process and securing an interview. Keeping up with the latest trends in technology and adapting to the changing recruitment landscape will undoubtedly give career changers an edge in their job search journey.

Optimizing Your Resume and Application for AI Screening

In today's job market, technology plays a significant role in the hiring process. With the rise of Artificial Intelligence (AI) screening tools, it is crucial for career changers to understand how to optimize their resume and application to increase their chances of landing an interview in 2024 and beyond.

AI screening tools are designed to streamline the hiring process by filtering out resumes that do not meet specific criteria. These tools rely on algorithms to scan resumes and identify keywords, skills, and qualifications that match the job description. As a career changer, it is essential to ensure that your resume stands out and effectively communicates your relevant skills and experiences to AI screening tools.

To optimize your resume for AI screening, start by carefully reviewing the job description and identifying the keywords and skills that are most relevant to the position. Incorporate these keywords throughout your resume, particularly in the summary, skills, and work experience sections. However, be mindful of striking a balance – ensure that your resume still reads naturally and is not overloaded with keywords.

Additionally, focus on highlighting transferable skills and experiences that demonstrate your adaptability and ability to succeed in a new career field. Emphasize any relevant certifications, training programs, or projects that showcase your commitment to learning and growth.

Apart from resume optimization, it is equally important to optimize your application as a whole. Pay attention to the application format and ensure that it is compatible with the AI screening tools used by the company. Stick to industry-standard formats like PDF or Word documents to avoid any formatting issues or compatibility errors.

Moreover, personalize your application by tailoring your cover letter to the specific job and company. Use this opportunity to explain your motivation for changing careers, highlight relevant experiences, and demonstrate your passion for the industry. By showcasing your dedication and genuine interest, you can make a lasting impression on both AI screening tools and human recruiters.

Lastly, regularly update and refine your resume and application materials to stay current with evolving AI screening technology. Stay informed about the latest trends and best practices in resume optimization, and adapt your strategy accordingly.

Optimizing your resume and application for AI screening is crucial for career changers looking to secure interviews in 2024 and beyond. By incorporating relevant keywords, highlighting transferable skills, and personalizing your application, you can increase your chances of standing out to both AI screening tools and human recruiters. Stay proactive, stay informed, and crack the 2024 interview code.

Leveraging AI Platforms for Interview Preparation

In the fast-paced and ever-evolving world of job interviews, staying ahead of the curve is crucial for career changers. With the advent of artificial intelligence (AI), the landscape of interviewing in 2024 is vastly different from what it used to be. In this subchapter, we will explore how career changers can leverage AI platforms for interview preparation, giving them a competitive edge and increasing their chances of success.

AI platforms have revolutionized the way interviews are conducted. These platforms utilize advanced algorithms to analyze data, predict trends, and provide personalized feedback. By embracing these technologies, career changers can benefit from a range of features designed to enhance their interview skills and confidence.

One key advantage of AI platforms is their ability to simulate real interview scenarios. Through virtual interviews, candidates can practice answering questions in a realistic setting, gaining valuable experience and identifying areas for improvement. These platforms often come equipped with facial recognition software, which captures and analyzes non-verbal cues, helping candidates refine their body language and communication skills.

Additionally, AI platforms offer personalized feedback based on performance analysis. By analyzing speech patterns, vocabulary, and tone of voice, these platforms can provide valuable insights into areas that need attention. Whether it's improving clarity, reducing filler words, or enhancing overall delivery, this feedback allows career changers to fine-tune their interview techniques and present themselves in the best possible light.

Furthermore, AI platforms can help candidates anticipate the types of questions they may encounter during interviews. By analyzing vast databases of interview questions and their corresponding answers, these platforms can provide comprehensive lists of potential questions tailored to specific industries or roles. Armed with this knowledge, career changers can prepare thoughtful and relevant responses, demonstrating their understanding of the industry and their suitability for the position.

AI platforms also provide access to extensive resources and materials for interview preparation. From articles on industry-specific trends to sample answers for frequently asked questions, these platforms offer a wealth of information to help career changers navigate the complexities of the job market. Furthermore, some platforms offer interactive tutorials and courses that provide guidance on various aspects of the interview process, from dressing professionally to negotiating job offers.

Leveraging AI platforms for interview preparation is a game-changer for career changers in 2024. These platforms offer realistic simulations, personalized feedback, question analysis, and access to valuable resources, all of which contribute to enhancing interview skills and increasing the chances of success. By embracing these technologies, career changers can confidently navigate the ever-evolving interview landscape and secure their dream jobs.

Demonstrating Your Skills and Abilities to AI Interviewers

As a career changer in the year 2024, you are likely to encounter a new and exciting development in the job market - AI interviewers. Companies have started utilizing artificial intelligence to streamline their hiring processes, making it essential for job seekers to adapt and learn how to effectively demonstrate their skills and abilities to these digital interviewers.

AI interviewers are designed to analyze and evaluate your responses based on predetermined criteria. They are trained to identify specific keywords, phrases, and patterns in your answers, which can determine whether you move forward in the hiring process. To succeed in this new era of interviewing, it is crucial to understand how to navigate these AI systems.

First and foremost, preparation is key. Research the company and the job role you are applying for to gain a deep understanding of the required skills and competencies. Then, tailor your responses to include relevant keywords and phrases that align with these requirements. By doing so, you increase your chances of catching the attention of the AI interviewer.

During the interview, be concise and provide clear examples of your skills and abilities. AI interviewers prefer structured responses that directly address the question at hand. Use the STAR method (Situation, Task, Action, Result) to structure your answers and showcase your problem-solving abilities. Highlight your achievements and quantify them whenever possible, as this helps the AI system recognize your accomplishments.

Additionally, it is important to remember that AI interviewers are programmed to analyze not only your words but also your non-verbal cues. Pay attention to your body language, facial expressions, and tone of voice. Practice good eye contact and maintain a confident posture to create a positive impression.

To further enhance your chances of success, optimize your resume and online presence for AI systems. Use industry-specific keywords and phrases throughout your resume, ensuring that your skills and experiences are easily recognizable by AI algorithms. Additionally, update your LinkedIn profile and other professional platforms to reflect the skills and achievements that align with the job you are applying for.

As a career changer, it is natural to feel apprehensive about AI interviewers. However, by thoroughly preparing, tailoring your responses, and optimizing your application materials, you can effectively demonstrate your skills and abilities to these digital interviewers. Embrace this new era of interviewing, and let your potential shine through the AI algorithms. Good luck on your career change journey!

Chapter 5
Cracking the Behavioral Interview Code

Analyzing Common Behavioral Interview Questions

In the ever-evolving world of job interviews, the importance of mastering behavioral questions cannot be emphasized enough. As a career changer, you may find yourself facing unique challenges when it comes to interviewing in 2024. However, with the right knowledge and preparation, you can crack the interview code and land the job of your dreams. This subchapter will provide you with insights into analyzing common behavioral interview questions, enabling you to navigate the interview process with confidence and success.

Behavioral interview questions are designed to assess your past experiences and behaviors to predict your future performance. They aim to understand how you handle various situations, adapt to change, and collaborate with others. In 2024, employers are increasingly relying on these questions to gauge a candidate's competencies and cultural fit within their organizations.

To effectively analyze behavioral questions, it is crucial to understand the different types that may be asked during an interview. Questions related to teamwork, problem-solving, leadership, and adaptability are some of the common categories you may encounter. By identifying these themes, you can anticipate the types of questions you may face and prepare accordingly.

In addition to recognizing the categories, it is essential to develop a structured approach to answering behavioral questions. The STAR (Situation, Task, Action, Result) method is widely recommended for organizing your responses. This method allows you to provide a concise and comprehensive answer by outlining the situation or problem, the task at hand, the action you took, and the result or outcome.

Another crucial aspect of analyzing behavioral questions is to understand the underlying qualities employers are seeking. While each question may have a specific focus, employers are often looking for traits such as resilience, adaptability, problem-solving skills, and the ability to work well in a team. By recognizing these underlying qualities, you can tailor your responses to highlight your strengths in these areas.

To further enhance your preparation, consider practicing with mock interviews and seeking feedback from professionals in your desired field. This will help you refine your answers, build confidence, and identify areas for improvement.

As a career changer, mastering the art of analyzing common behavioral interview questions is essential for your success in 2024. By understanding the different types of questions, adopting a structured approach, and highlighting the desired qualities, you can position yourself as a strong candidate in the competitive job market. With diligent preparation and practice, you will be well-equipped to crack the interview code and secure the career change you've been working towards.

Crafting Effective STAR Responses

In today's competitive job market, mastering the art of interviewing is crucial for career changers. As we enter the year 2024, the interview landscape has evolved, requiring candidates to adapt their strategies and techniques to stand out from the crowd. One technique that has proven to be highly effective is the use of STAR responses.

The STAR method is a structured approach to answering behavioral interview questions. It stands for Situation, Task, Action, and Result. By following this framework, career changers can effectively showcase their skills, experiences, and accomplishments in a concise and impactful manner.

To craft an effective STAR response, start by identifying a specific situation or challenge you encountered in your previous role. Clearly explain the context, including the industry, company, and your position. Then, outline the task or objective you were assigned and the expectations set for you.

Next, focus on the action you took to address the situation. Highlight the skills and competencies you utilized, explaining your thought process and decision-making. Be sure to emphasize any innovative or creative approaches you employed to overcome obstacles.

Finally, share the result of your actions. Quantify the outcome whenever possible, whether it's a percentage increase in sales, cost savings, or customer satisfaction ratings. Highlight the impact your actions had on the organization and how it contributed to achieving broader goals.

When crafting STAR responses, it's essential to keep in mind the specific challenges and trends of interviewing in 2024. Employers are increasingly seeking candidates who can demonstrate adaptability, resilience, and problem-solving abilities in the face of rapid technological advancements.

To make your STAR responses even more effective, consider incorporating relevant technical skills or industry-specific knowledge that align with the demands of your target role. This will demonstrate your commitment to staying up-to-date with industry trends and your ability to quickly learn and apply new information.

Practice your STAR responses before your interviews to ensure they flow naturally and concisely. Rehearse with a friend or mentor, seeking feedback on your delivery and impact. Remember, the goal is to provide compelling evidence of your abilities and accomplishments, leaving a lasting impression on the interviewer.

Crafting effective STAR responses is a powerful technique for career changers navigating the interview process in 2024. By following the structured approach and incorporating industry-specific knowledge, you can effectively showcase your skills and experiences, increasing your chances of securing your desired role in a new field.

Showcasing Transferable Skills and Experience

In the fast-paced and ever-evolving job market of 2024, career changers face unique challenges when it comes to interviewing. Employers are increasingly seeking candidates who can bring a diverse range of skills and experiences to the table. To stand out from the competition, it is crucial for career changers to effectively showcase their transferable skills and experiences during the interview process.

Transferable skills are abilities and knowledge that can be applied across different roles and industries. They are highly valuable for career changers as they demonstrate adaptability, versatility, and a willingness to learn. When preparing for an interview, it is vital to identify and highlight these skills to show prospective employers that you are the right fit for the job, despite coming from a different background.

One effective way to showcase transferable skills is by drawing connections between your previous experiences and the requirements of the new role. For example, if you are transitioning from a project management role to a marketing position, you can emphasize your ability to manage budgets, coordinate teams, and meet deadlines. These skills are applicable in both fields and demonstrate your capacity to adapt and excel in a new environment.

Additionally, career changers should focus on demonstrating their passion and motivation for the industry they are entering. Employers want to see that you have taken the time to understand the new field and have a genuine interest in it. Highlight any relevant courses, certifications, or volunteer work that you have undertaken to further develop your skills and knowledge in the new industry.

Another powerful strategy is to showcase any achievements and successes from your previous career that are applicable to the new role. Even if the achievements are not directly related to the industry you are entering, they demonstrate qualities such as leadership, problem-solving, and resilience, which are highly sought after by employers.

Furthermore, networking and seeking informational interviews can be incredibly beneficial for career changers. By connecting with professionals in the field you are transitioning into, you can gain insights, advice, and potentially even referrals. These interactions can provide you with valuable information that can be used to further showcase your transferable skills and experiences during interviews.

Showcasing transferable skills and experiences is crucial for career changers in the competitive job market of 2024. By effectively highlighting your abilities, passion, and achievements, you can demonstrate to employers that you are the ideal candidate, despite coming from a different background. Embrace your unique journey and use it as a strength to make a successful transition into a new career.

Handling Situational and Hypothetical Questions

In the ever-evolving landscape of job interviews, it is crucial for career changers to be well-prepared for the challenges that lie ahead. One of the most common types of questions you may encounter during an interview in 2024 are situational and hypothetical questions. These questions are designed to assess your problem-solving skills, critical thinking abilities, and how well you can handle potential challenges in the workplace.

Situational questions often present a hypothetical scenario and ask you to explain how you would respond or handle the situation. These questions aim to evaluate your ability to think on your feet and adapt to different circumstances. To effectively handle situational questions, it is important to follow a structured approach. Start by carefully listening to the question, ensuring you understand the scenario presented. Then, analyze the situation and consider the possible options or strategies you could employ. Next, clearly communicate your thought process and rationale behind your chosen approach. Lastly, conclude by summarizing the potential outcomes or benefits of your proposed solution.

Hypothetical questions, on the other hand, are designed to assess your ability to think critically and make informed decisions. These questions may ask you to consider a hypothetical scenario and provide your opinion or recommendation. When faced with a hypothetical question, take a moment to gather your thoughts and consider the different perspectives involved. Clearly state your opinion, supporting it with logical reasoning and any relevant experiences or knowledge you possess. Remember to remain calm, confident, and concise in your response.

To excel in handling situational and hypothetical questions during your interview in 2024, it is essential to prepare in advance. Research common interview scenarios and practice formulating well-thought-out answers to various hypothetical questions. Consider seeking assistance from career coaches or mentors who can provide valuable feedback and guidance. Additionally, stay updated on current industry trends and news to enhance your ability to provide relevant and up-to-date responses.

As a career changer, mastering the art of handling situational and hypothetical questions is crucial for interview success in 2024. By following a structured approach, staying calm and confident, and preparing thoroughly, you can effectively showcase your problem-solving skills and critical thinking abilities. Remember, practice makes perfect, so invest time and effort in honing your skills to crack the 2024 interview code and secure your dream career.

Chapter 6
Showcasing Your Value through Case Studies and Simulations

The Role of Case Studies and Simulations in Interviews

In the rapidly evolving job market of 2024, interviews have become more complex, requiring candidates to showcase not only their skills and qualifications but also their problem-solving abilities and adaptability. As a career changer, it is crucial to understand and prepare for the role that case studies and simulations play in interviews today.

Case studies are real or hypothetical scenarios that candidates are presented with during interviews. They require candidates to analyze the situation, identify the problem, and propose potential solutions. Case studies provide employers with valuable insights into a candidate's critical thinking, decision-making, and problem-solving skills. They also allow employers to assess a candidate's ability to apply their knowledge and experience to practical situations.

Simulations, on the other hand, are interactive exercises that simulate real work scenarios. They can range from role-playing exercises to virtual simulations on computers. Simulations provide employers with a glimpse into how candidates perform under pressure and in real-time situations. They allow candidates to showcase their communication skills, teamwork, and ability to handle complex tasks. Simulations are particularly beneficial for career changers as they provide an opportunity to demonstrate transferable skills and adaptability to new roles and industries.

To excel in interviews that involve case studies and simulations, career changers must prepare thoroughly. Start by researching the industry and role you are pursuing. Familiarize yourself with common challenges and trends. This knowledge will help you analyze case studies and simulations effectively.

Next, practice solving case studies and participating in simulations. Seek out resources online, such as industry-specific case studies or virtual simulations. Additionally, consider joining professional groups or networking events where you can participate in mock case studies or simulations. These opportunities will not only enhance your problem-solving abilities but also build your confidence in handling such interview scenarios.

During interviews, when faced with a case study or simulation, remain calm and focused. Take a moment to understand the problem, ask clarifying questions if necessary, and then outline your approach. Remember to think aloud, explaining your thought process to the interviewer. This will demonstrate your analytical skills and decision-making abilities.

Finally, be open to feedback and learn from each experience. If you encounter challenges during case studies or simulations, reflect on what you could have done differently and apply those learnings to future opportunities.

Case studies and simulations have become integral components of interviews in 2024. As a career changer, embracing these interview formats and preparing effectively will significantly enhance your chances of success. By honing your problem-solving skills, adaptability, and ability to think on your feet, you will position yourself as a standout candidate in today's competitive job market.

Understanding the Purpose and Format of Case Studies

In the rapidly evolving job market of 2024, the interview process has also undergone significant changes. As career changers, it is crucial to be well-prepared for the new interviewing techniques that employers are using. One such technique that has gained prominence in recent years is the case study.

A case study is an in-depth examination of a real-life situation or problem that an organization has faced. It provides a detailed analysis of the challenges, solutions, and outcomes of a specific scenario. Employers use case studies during interviews to assess a candidate's problem-solving skills, critical thinking abilities, and decision-making capabilities.

The purpose of a case study is not to find a definitive answer but to evaluate how an individual approaches complex problems and arrives at logical conclusions. It allows employers to gauge a candidate's ability to analyze data, think creatively, and make informed decisions under pressure. By presenting a real-world situation, case studies provide a glimpse into how candidates would handle similar challenges in the workplace.

In terms of format, case studies typically follow a structured approach. They begin by outlining the background of the situation, including relevant facts, figures, and any constraints or limitations. This is followed by a clear statement of the problem or objective that needs to be addressed. Candidates are then expected to analyze the available information, identify potential solutions, and present their recommendations.

During an interview, candidates may be given a case study to review and analyze in advance, or they may be presented with a case study on the spot and given a specific amount of time to prepare their response. It is important to familiarize yourself with both approaches and practice your analytical skills to ensure you can perform well under either circumstance.

To excel in case study interviews, career changers should develop a structured approach to problem-solving. This involves carefully reading and understanding the case study, identifying the key issues, brainstorming potential solutions, and evaluating the pros and cons of each option. It is crucial to articulate your thought process clearly and concisely, explaining the rationale behind your recommendations.

In conclusion, as a career changer interviewing in 2024, it is important to understand the purpose and format of case studies. These exercises allow employers to assess your problem-solving abilities and decision-making skills. By practicing your analytical thinking, developing a structured approach, and effectively communicating your thought process, you can confidently navigate case study interviews and increase your chances of success in your career transition.

Approaching Case Studies with Confidence and Analytical Thinking

As a career changer, the prospect of interviewing in 2024 might seem daunting. The job market is constantly evolving, and employers are increasingly relying on case studies during the interview process to assess a candidate's problem-solving skills and analytical thinking. However, with the right approach and mindset, you can navigate these challenges and stand out as a strong candidate.

In this subchapter, we will explore strategies to approach case studies with confidence and analytical thinking. By following these tips, you will be well-prepared to tackle any case study thrown your way during an interview.

First and foremost, it's crucial to understand the purpose of case studies in interviews. Employers use case studies to evaluate your ability to think critically, analyze complex problems, and propose effective solutions. They want to see how you approach and break down a problem, identify key issues, and develop a logical framework to solve it.

To excel in case studies, you must practice active listening and ask clarifying questions. Take the time to fully comprehend the problem at hand before jumping into a solution. This demonstrates your ability to grasp the nuances of the situation and ensures that you are addressing the right issues.

Analytical thinking is another key aspect of approaching case studies. Break down the problem into smaller components, identify the underlying patterns or trends, and gather relevant data to support your analysis. Employers want to see that you can think analytically and make evidence-based decisions.

Moreover, it's important to showcase your creativity and ability to think outside the box. While analytical thinking is crucial, employers also value innovative ideas and unique perspectives. Don't be afraid to propose unconventional solutions or challenge existing assumptions. This will demonstrate your ability to think critically and bring fresh ideas to the table.

Lastly, practice, practice, practice! Seek out case study resources, such as books or online platforms, and solve as many case studies as you can. This will help you become familiar with different types of problems and develop a structured approach to solving them. Additionally, consider participating in case study competitions or joining study groups to gain valuable feedback and insights from others.

Approaching case studies with confidence and analytical thinking is a skill that can be developed with practice and the right mindset. By following these strategies, you will be well-equipped to excel in the interview process as a career changer in 2024. Remember to stay calm, think critically, and trust in your problem-solving abilities. Good luck!

Demonstrating Problem-Solving Skills through Simulations

Subchapter - Demonstrating Problem-Solving Skills through Simulations

In today's rapidly changing job market, career changers face unique challenges when it comes to interviewing in 2024. Employers are increasingly interested in candidates who possess problem-solving skills and the ability to think critically in real-life scenarios. One effective way to showcase these skills is through simulations during the interview process. This subchapter will explore how career changers can demonstrate problem-solving abilities through simulations and ace their interviews in 2024.

Simulations are realistic scenarios designed to mimic actual work situations. They provide interviewers with a glimpse into how candidates approach problems, make decisions, and collaborate with others. By participating in simulations, career changers can showcase their problem-solving skills and prove their adaptability to new roles and industries.

To excel in simulations, it is crucial for career changers to thoroughly research the company and the specific role they are applying for. This knowledge will help them understand the challenges they may face and allow them to propose effective solutions during the simulation. Additionally, career changers should familiarize themselves with the industry's latest trends and best practices to ensure they bring relevant insights to the simulation.

During the simulation, career changers should focus on actively listening, thinking critically, and communicating their thought process clearly. They must demonstrate their ability to analyze complex problems, break them down into manageable components, and propose innovative solutions. It is essential to showcase adaptability and flexibility, as these traits are highly valued in an ever-evolving job market.

To stand out, career changers should also emphasize their transferable skills gained from previous experiences. By drawing connections between their past achievements and the problem at hand, they can demonstrate how their unique perspective and diverse background can contribute to the organization's success.

Furthermore, collaboration is a key aspect of problem-solving. Career changers should showcase their ability to work effectively in teams, leverage the strengths of others, and build consensus to reach the best outcome. This will highlight their interpersonal skills and their capacity to navigate diverse work environments.

Simulations offer career changers a valuable opportunity to demonstrate their problem-solving skills during interviews in 2024. By thoroughly preparing, conducting industry research, and showcasing their transferable skills, career changers can impress interviewers with their ability to think critically, adapt, and collaborate effectively. Embracing simulations as part of the interview process can significantly increase their chances of success in securing a new career path.

Chapter 7
Nailing the Final Interview and Negotiating Offers

Preparing for the Final Interview Round

Congratulations, career changers! You have made it to the final interview round, an exciting milestone in your journey towards a new career. This subchapter will guide you through the necessary steps to ensure you are fully prepared for this crucial stage.

Interviewing in 2024 presents unique challenges and opportunities. With rapidly evolving technology and a competitive job market, it is important to stay ahead of the curve. Here are some essential tips to help you crack the final interview code and land your dream job -

1. Research the Company - In the digital age, information is readily available. Dive deep into the company's website, social media platforms, and news articles to understand its mission, values, recent achievements, and challenges. This knowledge will impress the interviewers and demonstrate your genuine interest in the organization.

2. Understand the Role - Review the job description once again and identify the key responsibilities and requirements. Match your skills and experiences with what the company is seeking. Be prepared to explain how your unique background as a career changer makes you a valuable asset for the position.

3. Practice, Practice, Practice - Mock interviews are a great way to gain confidence and refine your responses. Enlist the help of a friend, family member, or career coach to conduct practice sessions. Focus on articulating your career change story, highlighting relevant achievements, and answering common interview questions.

4. Showcase Transferable Skills - As a career changer, emphasize your transferable skills that are applicable to the new role. For example, if you are transitioning from sales to marketing, highlight your communication, negotiation, and relationship-building skills. Demonstrate how these skills can contribute to your success in the new position.

5. Prepare Thoughtful Questions - During the final interview, you will likely have the opportunity to ask questions. Prepare a list of thoughtful and insightful questions about the company, team dynamics, and growth opportunities. This demonstrates your enthusiasm and engagement in the potential role.

6. Leverage Technology - In 2024, technology plays a crucial role in the interview process. Familiarize yourself with video interviewing platforms and practice using them. Ensure your internet connection, microphone, and camera are working properly. Dress professionally, even for virtual interviews, as this will help you project a confident and capable image.

Remember, the final interview round is your chance to shine and convince the hiring team that you are the right candidate for the job. By conducting thorough research, showcasing your transferable skills, and practicing your interview techniques, you can crack the 2024 interview code and secure your desired career change. Good luck!

Showcasing Your Fit with the Company Culture

In the ever-evolving job market of 2024, one of the key factors that can make or break your success in an interview is showcasing your fit with the company culture. As a career changer, it is essential to understand the importance of aligning your values and personality traits with the organization you are applying to.

Company culture refers to the shared values, beliefs, and practices that define an organization and its employees. It encompasses everything from the way people communicate and collaborate to the organization's mission, vision, and work environment. Employers are increasingly recognizing the significance of a strong cultural fit in ensuring employee satisfaction, productivity, and long-term success.

To showcase your fit with the company culture during an interview, you must first research and understand the organization's values and work environment. This can be done through various channels such as the company's website, social media platforms, and online reviews. By familiarizing yourself with their culture, you can tailor your responses to highlight your compatibility.

When discussing your fit with the company culture, it is essential to emphasize your alignment with the organization's values. Highlight experiences from your past career that demonstrate your commitment to those values and how they align with the company's mission. For instance, if the organization values innovation and creativity, discuss a project where you took an innovative approach to solve a problem.

Moreover, showcase your adaptability and willingness to learn new skills. As a career changer, you bring a unique perspective and a diverse skill set to the table. Emphasize how your previous experiences have prepared you to adapt to different work environments and how you have successfully navigated through change.

Additionally, during the interview, pay attention to nonverbal cues and the overall atmosphere of the organization. This will help you gauge if the company culture aligns with your own values and preferences. Remember, the interview is not just an opportunity for the employer to assess you; it is also your chance to evaluate if the organization is the right fit for you.

Showcasing your fit with the company culture is crucial for career changers in the competitive job market of 2024. By aligning your values, emphasizing your adaptability, and demonstrating your compatibility with the organization's mission, you can increase your chances of success in the interview process. Remember, finding the right cultural fit is not just about getting a job; it is about finding a workplace where you can thrive and grow.

Handling Salary Negotiations and Benefits Discussions

In the ever-evolving job market of 2024, career changers face unique challenges when it comes to interviewing. Among these challenges is the delicate task of handling salary negotiations and benefits discussions. In this subchapter, we will provide you with invaluable guidance on how to navigate these crucial aspects of the interview process, ensuring you secure the best possible compensation package for your new career.

1. Research and Preparation -

Before entering any salary negotiation or benefits discussion, thorough research is key. Familiarize yourself with industry standards, salary ranges, and benefits commonly offered in your desired field. This will provide you with a solid foundation for negotiations and enable you to have realistic expectations.

2. Be Confident and Assertive -

As a career changer, it's important to approach salary negotiations with confidence. Highlight the transferable skills and unique perspectives you bring to the table. Emphasize how your previous experience can add value to the company, making a strong case for a competitive salary. Be assertive, but also open to a constructive dialogue to find a mutually beneficial outcome.

3. Leverage Your Unique Selling Points -

Career changers often possess a diverse range of skills and experiences that can be leveraged during salary negotiations. Showcase how your transferable skills can positively impact the organization. Demonstrate your ability to adapt quickly and bring a fresh perspective to the role. Highlighting these unique selling points can add leverage to your negotiation position.

4. Negotiate Beyond the Salary -

While salary negotiations are essential, don't overlook the importance of discussing benefits. Inquire about health insurance plans, retirement contributions, vacation time, professional development opportunities, and any other perks that may be negotiable. Remember, a comprehensive benefits package can greatly enhance your overall compensation.

5. Stay Professional and Respectful -

Throughout the negotiation process, it is crucial to maintain a professional and respectful demeanor. Remember that negotiations are a collaborative effort, and maintaining a positive relationship with your potential employer is essential. Even if the initial offer isn't what you desired, avoid becoming confrontational or disheartened. Instead, focus on finding common ground and managing expectations.

By following these guidelines, you will be well-equipped to handle salary negotiations and benefits discussions in the fast-paced world of interviewing in 2024. Remember to remain confident, leverage your unique selling points, and maintain professionalism throughout the process. With the right approach, you can secure a compensation package that reflects your skills, experience, and the value you bring to your new career as a career changer.

Evaluating Multiple Offers and Making an Informed Decision

As a career changer in the year 2024, the job market is full of exciting opportunities. However, with numerous offers on the table, it can be challenging to evaluate them and make an informed decision. This subchapter aims to guide you through the process of evaluating multiple job offers and help you make the right career choice.

1. Assess your priorities - Before diving into the evaluation process, take a step back and reflect on your career goals and priorities. Consider factors such as work-life balance, growth opportunities, company culture, compensation, and location. By clarifying your priorities, you can easily compare offers based on what matters most to you.

2. Evaluate the job descriptions - Carefully review each job description and assess how well they align with your skills, experience, and interests. Look for clear responsibilities and potential for growth within the role. Consider whether the offered position will challenge and motivate you, or if it aligns with your long-term career goals.

3. Research the companies - Conduct thorough research on each company to gain insights into their values, reputation, and future prospects. Explore their websites, read reviews, and analyze their financial stability. Look for information on employee satisfaction, company growth, and any recent news or developments that might impact your decision.

4. Consider the compensation package - While salary is essential, it's not the only factor to consider. Evaluate the entire compensation package, including benefits, bonuses, stock options, and retirement plans. Assess the value of these benefits and how they align with your financial goals and personal needs.

5. Seek advice and gather information - Reach out to your network or professional contacts who might have knowledge or experience with the companies you are considering. Ask for their insights and opinions on the work environment, company culture, and growth opportunities. Their perspectives can provide valuable information that might not be readily available online.

6. Assess the potential for growth - Consider the opportunities for professional development and advancement within each company. Look for organizations that invest in their employees' growth through training programs, mentorship opportunities, or tuition reimbursement. A company that values and supports your development can significantly impact your long-term career trajectory.

7. Trust your instincts - Lastly, listen to your gut feeling. After weighing all the factors mentioned above, trust your intuition. If a particular offer resonates with you and aligns with your aspirations and values, it may be the right choice for you.

Remember, evaluating multiple job offers requires careful consideration and research. By following these steps and considering your priorities, you can make an informed decision that sets you on the path to a successful career change in 2024.

Chapter 8
Succeeding in the New Role and Beyond

Onboarding and Transitioning into the New Career

Starting a new career can be both exhilarating and overwhelming, especially for those who are making a career change. In this subchapter, we will discuss the importance of a smooth onboarding process and provide valuable insights on how to transition seamlessly into your new career in the year 2024.

The first step in any successful career transition is to understand the importance of onboarding. Onboarding is the process of integrating into a new work environment, familiarizing yourself with the company culture, and acquiring the necessary skills and knowledge to excel in your new role. It sets the foundation for your success and can significantly impact your overall job satisfaction.

In the year 2024, onboarding processes have evolved with the changing dynamics of the workplace. Virtual onboarding has become the norm, and companies are increasingly utilizing technology to facilitate a seamless transition. As a career changer, it is crucial to adapt and embrace these changes to make the most of your onboarding experience.

To ensure a smooth transition, it is essential to take proactive steps during the onboarding process. Research the company thoroughly before your start date to gain a better understanding of its values, mission, and culture. This will help you align yourself with the company's goals and values from day one.

Additionally, leverage your existing skills and experiences to your advantage. As a career changer, you bring a unique perspective and a diverse skill set to the table. Identify transferable skills that can be applied to your new role and communicate them effectively during the onboarding process.

Networking is another crucial aspect of transitioning into a new career. Connect with colleagues, mentors, and industry professionals who can provide guidance and support. Attend industry events, join professional groups, and participate in online forums to expand your network and stay updated with the latest trends in your field.

Onboarding and transitioning into a new career is a critical phase for career changers in 2024. Embrace virtual onboarding, invest time in researching the company, leverage your transferable skills, and build a strong network to ensure a successful transition. By following these steps, you will be well-prepared to navigate your new career path and excel in your chosen field.

Building Relationships and Establishing a Professional Network

In today's rapidly changing job market, building strong relationships and establishing a professional network is crucial, especially for career changers. As you navigate the landscape of interviewing in 2024, it is important to understand that a robust network can open doors to new opportunities and help you make a successful transition into your desired field.

One of the first steps in building relationships is to identify your target industry or niche. Research and gather information about the key players, organizations, and professionals within that field. This will help you create a solid foundation for networking.

Networking events and industry conferences are excellent opportunities to connect with like-minded professionals and expand your network. Make an effort to attend these events, engage with others, and exchange contact information. Remember, networking is not just about collecting business cards; it's about building meaningful relationships.

In the digital age, social media platforms play a significant role in networking. Utilize platforms like LinkedIn to connect with professionals in your target industry. Join relevant groups and actively participate in discussions to showcase your knowledge and expertise. Engage with others by commenting on their posts or sharing valuable insights. By doing so, you can establish yourself as a thought leader and attract the attention of potential employers or mentors.

Another effective way to build relationships is through informational interviews. Reach out to professionals in your desired industry and request a meeting to learn more about their experiences and insights. This not only helps you gain valuable knowledge but also allows you to create a connection with someone who may be able to provide guidance or refer you to job opportunities.

Additionally, volunteering or joining professional organizations related to your target industry can be immensely beneficial. These activities not only give you a chance to develop new skills but also provide opportunities to connect with professionals who share your interests and goals.

Remember, building relationships and establishing a professional network is a long-term process. It requires consistent effort and genuine interest in others. Be proactive in reaching out, maintaining contacts, and offering support when needed. Your network will be a valuable resource throughout your career, providing you with insights, mentorship, and potential job opportunities.

In conclusion, as a career changer interviewing in 2024, building relationships and establishing a professional network is essential for your success. By actively engaging in networking events, utilizing social media platforms, conducting informational interviews, and participating in relevant organizations, you can create a robust network that will support your transition into your desired field. Embrace the power of networking, and you will find doors opening and opportunities flowing your way.

Continuously Developing Skills and Knowledge

In the fast-paced and ever-evolving job market of 2024, the importance of continuously developing skills and knowledge cannot be overstated. As a career changer, you need to stay ahead of the game and adapt to the changing trends in order to successfully navigate the interview process.

Gone are the days when having a static set of skills would guarantee you a job. Employers in 2024 are seeking candidates who are not only proficient in their field but also possess a growth mindset and a hunger for learning. Therefore, it is crucial that you prioritize skill development and knowledge enhancement to stand out from the competition.

One of the key ways to continuously develop your skills and knowledge is to embrace lifelong learning. This means actively seeking out opportunities to learn new things, whether it's through attending workshops, enrolling in online courses, or joining professional networks. Stay updated on the latest industry trends and advancements, as this will give you an edge during interviews and demonstrate your commitment to professional growth.

Additionally, it is essential to become familiar with emerging technologies and their impact on your field. The job market in 2024 will be heavily influenced by automation, artificial intelligence, and data analytics. By proactively acquiring skills related to these areas, you will position yourself as a valuable asset to prospective employers.

Another effective method for skill development is to engage in practical experiences. Seek out internships, volunteer work, or freelance projects that allow you to apply your existing skills while also gaining new ones. These experiences not only provide you with valuable hands-on knowledge but also demonstrate your ability to adapt and learn quickly.

Furthermore, networking should not be underestimated when it comes to continuous skill development. Attend industry conferences, join professional associations, and connect with like-minded individuals who can offer insights and opportunities. Networking can expose you to new ideas, facilitate mentorship opportunities, and open doors to potential job leads.

As a career changer preparing for interviews in 2024, continuously developing your skills and knowledge is crucial. Embrace lifelong learning, stay updated on industry trends, and acquire skills related to emerging technologies. Engage in practical experiences and leverage networking opportunities to enhance your skill set further. By demonstrating your commitment to growth and adaptability, you will position yourself as a strong candidate and increase your chances of success in the competitive job market of 2024.

Embracing Lifelong Learning and Adaptability

In the rapidly evolving professional landscape of the 21st century, the importance of lifelong learning and adaptability cannot be overstated. As a career changer, understanding and embracing these qualities will not only help you navigate the challenging world of job interviews in 2024 but also set you up for long-term success in your new career.

The concept of lifelong learning goes beyond simply acquiring new knowledge and skills. It involves a mindset that promotes curiosity, continuous growth, and the willingness to embrace change. In today's job market, where technology advancements and industry trends can render skills obsolete in a matter of years, being a lifelong learner is essential.

When it comes to interviewing in 2024, employers will be seeking candidates who can demonstrate their adaptability. They will look for individuals who are not only open to change but who actively seek out opportunities to learn and grow. By showcasing your ability to adapt, you will prove to potential employers that you are capable of thriving in a dynamic and ever-changing work environment.

One way to demonstrate your commitment to lifelong learning is by staying up-to-date with the latest industry trends and advancements. Take advantage of online courses, webinars, and industry conferences to expand your knowledge and gain insights into the changes shaping your chosen field. Additionally, seek out networking opportunities with professionals in your target industry to stay informed about emerging trends and best practices.

Another vital aspect of embracing lifelong learning and adaptability is being willing to step outside your comfort zone. As a career changer, you may be entering a completely new industry or role. Embrace the unfamiliar and be open to taking on new challenges. Employers value candidates who show resilience and can quickly adapt to new environments.

In your job interviews, be prepared to discuss how you have embraced lifelong learning and adaptability in your career transition. Highlight specific instances where you have successfully adapted to change or learned new skills. Discuss how you proactively seek out opportunities for growth and how you stay updated with industry developments.

By emphasizing your commitment to lifelong learning and adaptability, you will position yourself as an attractive candidate for employers in 2024. Embrace change, stay curious, and be open to new experiences. In doing so, you will not only excel in your interviews but also thrive in your new career.

Chapter 9
Cracking the 2024 Interview Code

Reflecting on the Journey of Career Change

Embarking on a career change can be an exhilarating yet daunting journey. As career changers, we often find ourselves at a crossroads, questioning our decisions and feeling uncertain about the path ahead. However, it is in these moments of reflection that we truly discover our true potential and embrace the opportunities that lie ahead.

In this subchapter, "Reflecting on the Journey of Career Change," we delve deep into the experiences and insights of successful career changers who have cracked the code to interviewing in 2024. Their stories serve as a guiding light for those who are considering or in the midst of a career change, offering valuable lessons and inspiration.

One of the key aspects emphasized in this subchapter is the importance of self-reflection. Before diving into a new career, it is crucial to understand what motivates us, our strengths, and the skills we bring to the table. By taking the time to reflect on our journey, we gain a deeper understanding of our passions and align them with our desired career path.

Additionally, this subchapter highlights the significance of conducting thorough research and staying up-to-date with the latest trends in the job market. In 2024, the interviewing landscape is expected to be vastly different from previous years. Technology, remote working, and virtual interviews are set to become the norm. By staying informed and adapting to these changes, career changers can position themselves as valuable candidates in the job market.

Furthermore, the subchapter explores the power of networking and building meaningful connections. As career changers, we have the opportunity to tap into various networks and gain insights from professionals who have successfully transitioned into new fields. By expanding our network, we can uncover hidden job opportunities, gain mentorship, and receive invaluable advice to navigate the interview process in 2024.

Lastly, "Reflecting on the Journey of Career Change" emphasizes the importance of perseverance and resilience. Career changes can be met with setbacks and challenges, but it is through these obstacles that we grow and learn. By developing a growth mindset and embracing the journey, we can navigate the interview process with confidence and tenacity.

The subchapter "Reflecting on the Journey of Career Change" acts as a guiding compass for career changers in the year 2024. By reflecting on our journey, conducting thorough research, networking, and embracing resilience, we can crack the code to successful interviews and embark on a fulfilling career change. So, let us take a moment to reflect, learn, and thrive on this transformative journey.

Embracing the Skills and Strategies for Future Success

In the fast-paced world we live in, the job market is constantly evolving. As a career changer, it is essential to equip yourself with the skills and strategies necessary to succeed in the ever-changing landscape of interviewing in 2024 and beyond. This subchapter of "Cracking the 2024 Interview Code - A Guide for Career Changers" focuses on the key factors that will help you navigate this new era of job interviews.

1. Adaptability - One of the most crucial skills for career changers is adaptability. In the rapidly changing job market, employers are looking for candidates who can quickly learn and adjust to new environments. Embracing change and being open to acquiring new skills will set you apart from the competition.

2. Digital Literacy - Technology has reshaped the interview process. As a career changer, it is essential to be proficient in digital tools and platforms commonly used in today's job market. Be prepared to showcase your digital literacy skills during interviews, as employers increasingly rely on technology for communication and collaboration.

3. Emotional Intelligence - The ability to understand and manage emotions, both your own and others', is a valuable skill in the workplace. Employers are placing increasing importance on emotional intelligence when evaluating candidates. Develop your skills in areas such as empathy, self-awareness, and effective communication to demonstrate your emotional intelligence during interviews.

4. Transferable Skills - As a career changer, you may have a wealth of transferable skills that can be applied to your new field. Identify the skills you have gained from your previous experiences and highlight how they can benefit your potential employer. Emphasize your ability to adapt, problem-solve, and work in diverse teams to showcase your value.

5. Continuous Learning - In a rapidly changing job market, learning should not stop once you secure a new role. Demonstrating a commitment to continuous learning is essential for career changers. Showcase your willingness to learn new technologies, acquire new certifications, and stay updated on industry trends during interviews.

6. Networking - Building a strong professional network is crucial for career changers. Leverage your existing network and proactively seek opportunities to expand it. Networking can provide valuable insights, job leads, and mentorship opportunities that can help you navigate the interview process more effectively.

As a career changer, embracing these skills and strategies will position you for future success in the evolving job market of 2024. By focusing on adaptability, digital literacy, emotional intelligence, transferable skills, continuous learning, and networking, you will increase your chances of landing the job you desire. Stay proactive, stay curious, and keep evolving to crack the interview code of 2024 and beyond.

Continuing to Evolve in an Ever-Changing Job Market

In the fast-paced world of technology and globalization, the job market is constantly evolving. As a career changer, it is crucial to stay ahead of the curve and adapt to the ever-changing landscape of job interviews in 2024. This subchapter will explore key strategies and insights to help you navigate the interview process successfully.

1. Embrace the Digital Transformation - Technology has revolutionized the way companies conduct interviews. As a career changer, you must familiarize yourself with virtual interviews, video conferencing platforms, and online assessments. Practice using these tools to ensure a seamless and professional experience during your interviews.

2. Showcase Your Transferable Skills - Career changers often possess a unique set of skills that can be valuable in various industries. Highlight your transferable skills during interviews to demonstrate your versatility and adaptability. Emphasize how your previous experiences can contribute to the new role and explain how you have successfully transitioned in the past.

3. Continuous Learning and Upskilling - In a rapidly changing job market, employers value candidates who are committed to continuous learning. Showcase your dedication to professional development by mentioning relevant certifications, courses, or workshops you have completed. Discuss how you stay up-to-date with industry trends and demonstrate your willingness to adapt to new technologies and methodologies.

4. Research and Preparation - In 2024, employers expect candidates to be well-informed about their company, industry, and role. Take the time to thoroughly research the organization you are interviewing with, including their mission, values, recent projects, and competitors. This will not only demonstrate your interest but also help you tailor your answers to align with their objectives.

5. Soft Skills Are Key - While technical skills are essential, soft skills have become increasingly important in the modern workplace. Employers are looking for candidates who possess strong communication, problem-solving, and collaboration abilities. During interviews, provide specific examples of situations where you have effectively utilized these skills to achieve positive outcomes.

6. Adaptability and Resilience - The job market is unpredictable, and the ability to adapt and bounce back from setbacks is crucial. Highlight instances where you have demonstrated resilience and adaptability, such as successfully navigating through challenging projects or taking on new responsibilities outside of your comfort zone.

In 2024, it is vital to embrace the changing job market and equip yourself with the necessary skills and mindset to succeed in interviews. By staying up-to-date with technology, showcasing your transferable skills, emphasizing continuous learning, conducting thorough research, highlighting your soft skills, and demonstrating adaptability and resilience, you can maximize your chances of cracking the interview code and securing your dream role.